Cinco de Mayo

Celebrating the Traditions of Mexico

by Diane Hoyt-Goldsmith

photographs by Lawrence Migdale

Holiday House–New York

HOLIDAY HOUSE is registered in the U.S. Patent and Trademark Office.

3 5 7 9 10 8 6 4 2

Library of Congress Cataloging-in-Publication Data

Hoyt-Goldsmith, Diane.
Cinco de mayo: celebrating the traditions of Mexico / by Diane Hoyt-Goldsmith; photographs by Lawrence Migdale. —1st ed.
p. cm.
ISBN-13: 978-0-8234-2107-7 (hardcover)
ISBN-13: 978-0-8234-2279-1 (paperback)
1. Cinco de Mayo (Mexican holiday)—History—Juvenile literature. 2. Cinco de Mayo, Battle of, Puebla, Mexico, 1862—Juvenile literature. 3. Mexico—Social life and customs—Juvenile literature. I. Migdale, Lawrence, ill. II. Title.
F1233.H78 2007
394.262—dc22
2006101433

Acknowledgments
We are very grateful for the participation of many people to make this book possible, especially Rosalba Rosas and her entire family: Fernando, Concepción, Zoila, María, Gerardo, and her grandmother Josefa; Jesús, María, and Eric Arrizón; Ana Arrizón; Daniel Gavino; and Socorro Arrizón. Many thanks to Victor and his parents, Jim and Margarita Wilson, for their participation and help, and to Victor's brother Jessie and his grandparents Tomás and Teresa González.

Thanks also for the participation and advice of Eugene Rodríquez and the staff at Los Genzontles: Fabiola Trujillo, Lucina Rodríguez, Hugo Arroyo, Tregar Otton, Jorge Raya, and Sage Baggott. We are very grateful to Amanda Almonte for her advice and help in researching the project.

Los Genzontles began as a California Arts Council artist in residency in 1989 by Eugene Rodríguez and Berenice Zuniga-Yap. Their goal was to create a family-like environment for young people to learn and explore traditional Mexican music and dance. Today, Los Genzontles Mexican Arts Center continues to deepen and strengthen its programming, with a staff and much of the faculty comprised of local young people who have grown up in the program. The accomplishments of Los Genzontles Mexican Arts Center have not gone unheralded. Founding Director Eugene Rodríguez was recently chosen as an Arts Leadership Fellow by the National Arts Strategies and the Stanford Graduate School of Business Center for Social Innovation. In 2002 Los Genzontles Mexican Arts Center was a recipient of the Coming Up Taller Awards made by the Presidential Committee on Arts and Humanities, and in November 2002 Eugene Rodríguez received a Director's Award from the California Arts Council for outstanding leadership in the arts. Los Genzontles Mexican Arts Center has been recognized with a Profiles of Excellence Award from KGO Television, a Familias Unidas Award for Cultura Real, and a La Promesa Award from the National Latino Children's Agenda, receiving the highest ranking in the nation for excellence in Latino children's programs. Through the work of Los Genzontles Touring Group—which undertook a successful tour (Cuatro Maestros) to seven California communities in Summer 2001 and embarked on an international research-performance project in collaboration with Radio Bilingüe in 2003—Los Genzontles Mexican Arts Center has become recognized on both sides of the border as an important center for the research, preservation, and dissemination of traditional Mexican culture. For those interested in finding traditional mariachi music as well as documentary films about the traditional music of Mexico, CDs and DVDs are available through the Web site: www.loscenzontles.com. Los Genzontles CDs can be purchased online or by calling toll free to (866) 364-7887. Los Genzontles CDs are also available for download on iTunes® and other music download sites. Documentary Film Series: *Pasajero, A Journey of Time and Memory, Fandango, Searching for the White Monkey*. Traditional Mexican Music CDs: *Plan de la Villa: Traditional Mariachi*, Volume 1. With Julián González, *El Pasajero: Traditional Mariachi*, Volume II. With Julián González, *El Chivo Traditional Mariachi*, Volume III: features rarely heard *sones, rancheras, corridos,* and marches in the rural style of Jalisco, Mexico; *El Toro Viejo Traditional Mariachi*, Volume IV: fourth—and finest—volume of little-known traditional mariachi songs and dances; *Media Vida*, a collection of *rancheras, sones jarochos, pirecuas,* and more; *Cuatro Maestros*, featuring Los Genzontles with Santiago Jiménez Jr. of San Antonio, Texas; Andrés Vega of Grupo Mono Blanco of Veracruz; Julián González of Tecolotlán, Jalisco; and Atilano López of Jaracuaro, Michoacán; *Hypnotizada: Banda de Aire Estilo de Sinaloa*; *Volando en los Cafetales, sones jarochos*: traditional music of Veracruz.

In addition, we had the expert guidance of a wonderful traditional musician, Julián González Saldaña, *el mariachi*. Julián was born in Camichines, Jalisco, and raised in a rural hacienda. Don Julián plays violin, sings, and dances. He learned music from his father and the music elders of the ranch in an environment of the parties that followed long harvests in the cane fields. In 1997 he, along with other rural musicians, formed Mariachi Los Centenarios in order to compete in the fifth Encuentro Mundial de Mariachi, Guadalajara, Mexico. There they took second place in the category of the traditional mariachi, which plays without trumpets, a modern addition to the mariachi. Julián was recently awarded a master/apprenticeship grant by the California Traditional Arts Advancement Program to work with members of Los Genzontles.

Thanks also to the staff and customers of El Provenir in San Pablo, California: Fernando Rosas, Donato Rosas, Bernardo Rosas, Jaime Rosas, José Luiz Rojas, Jesús Enrique Díaz Aarrecia, Jesús Ávila Duarte, Ana Almanza Gutiérrez, Victoria Hernández Ernesto, Raymondo Hernández, and Ana González.

We are grateful to Toby's Feed Barn in Point Reyes and to Dolores Gonzáles and the children of the West Marin School for their participation in the Cinco de Mayo fiesta. And it wouldn't be Cinco de Mayo without a parade. Thanks to the folks who sponsor the parade in San Jose, Abel Cota and Letetia Rodríguez of the American GI Forum of San Jose, California, and to Folklórico Nacional Juvenil de Elena Robles for their participation.

Thanks to Andrés and Betty Garza for their help in researching this project; to Valerie Slovan; and especially to Terry Lowenthal for her skills in Photoshop.

The Alvarado Adobe is a replica of the home that Governor Juan Bautista Alvarado lived in during the 1840s, when California was a part of Mexico.

Rosalba Rosas lives in Hercules, California, near San Francisco. Everyone calls her Rosie. Rosie's parents are both from Mexico, but she and her four older brothers and sisters were born in the United States. Every May, Rosie and her family celebrate Cinco de Mayo, an important date in Mexican history. It is a time to take pride in Mexican traditions and share them with others in the community.

What Is Cinco de Mayo?

Many people think that Cinco de Mayo is a celebration of Mexico's independence—but it is not. For hundreds of years, Mexico was a colony of Spain, winning its independence in 1821. Mexicans celebrate their independence each year on September 16 with a national holiday.

Cinco de Mayo celebrates something that happened forty-one years after independence. In Spanish, *cinco de Mayo* means "fifth of May." It was on this date in 1862 that the Mexican army defeated the French in a decisive battle in the town of Puebla, Mexico.

Why was the French army so far from home, invading a country on the other side of the Atlantic Ocean? At that time, France, along with England and Spain, had made loans to the Mexican government. Mexico couldn't afford to pay the money back right away. The Mexican president Benito Juárez suspended repayment of the debts for several years because the country was bankrupt.

Unfortunately, the governments of England, Spain, and France did not want to wait to be repaid. These countries sent warships full of troops to Veracruz on Mexico's east coast and prepared to launch an invasion.

(Above) This map of Mexico shows the locations of Veracruz, Puebla, and Mexico City.

(Right) A cannon in the ruins of Fort Loreto in Puebla is a reminder of the battle that was fought there.

President Benito Juárez reached an agreement with both Spain and England, and their ships soon departed. But the French army, which at that time was considered one of the strongest in the world, remained. French soldiers began to march toward the capital, Mexico City.

On May 5, 6,000 French soldiers reached the town of Puebla, just one hundred miles from Mexico City. On the hills above the town, 4,500 Mexican soldiers were garrisoned in Fort Loreto and Fort Guadalupe. The Mexican army, led by General Ignacio Zaragoza, was aided by a small group of native people. These untrained fighters were armed only with old-fashioned rifles, farm tools, and machetes. The battle lasted for less than a day. When it was over, and against all odds, the Mexicans had won.

In spite of their success in Puebla, however, the Mexican army was not strong enough to push the French invaders out of the country. Eventually, the French army was successful. Emperor Maximilian of Austria, who was a relative of the French leader Napoleon, was put in place as the ruler of Mexico.

Maximilian's government did not last long. The victory at Puebla gave the people of Mexico confidence to resist the French. Four years later, under the leadership of President Juárez, the Mexicans defeated the French and drove them from their country.

Cinco de Mayo is an important holiday in Mexico. To celebrate, some communities near Puebla sponsor a reenactment of the battle—complete with period costumes, horses, and replicas of the rifles and machetes that were used long ago. Even today, the victory of Cinco de Mayo remains a strong symbol of the desire of the Mexican people to be independent.

Many cities in Mexico have a street named for the battle of Cinco de Mayo. Calle 5 de Mayo in Puebla is a popular shopping street.

On the Mexican flag, green represents Hope, white stands for Purity, and red represents Union.

The image in the center of the Mexican flag is a symbol of Mexico's Aztec heritage.

A legend says that the gods told the Aztecs to build a great city where they found an eagle, perched on a cactus, eating a snake.

The Aztecs saw this mythical eagle on the shores of a large lake. There they founded the great city of Tenochtitlan.

Today the zócalo, or main plaza, in Mexico City occupies the place of the ruined Aztec city.

Benito Juárez
President of Mexico
(1806–1872)

Born—March 21, 1806—San Pablo Guelatao, Oaxaca
Died—July 18, 1872—Distrito Federal, México

Benito Juárez, who was president of Mexico during the battle at Puebla, is often compared with American president Abraham Lincoln. Both men were born to poor families but rose to become great leaders. Both governed their nations at a time of war and strife. Both helped shape the future of their nations. Sadly, each of these great leaders died while serving his country as president—Abraham Lincoln was killed by an assassin's bullet, and Benito Juárez suffered a heart attack while working at his desk.

In nineteenth-century Mexico, society was divided into three main groups. At the top were the *criollos,* who were born in Mexico of Spanish parents. They were the wealthiest people. In the middle were the *mestizos*, people of mixed Spanish and native parents. The poorest of all were the native people, *los indígenas*, whose ancestors had lived in Mexico for many thousands of years.

Benito Juárez was a native Mexican, born in a small pueblo near Oaxaca. Orphaned before his fourth birthday, he was raised by his grandparents and an uncle. He spent his youth working in the cornfields and watching over his uncle's sheep.

When Benito was twelve years old, he walked from his village to the city of Oaxaca, where his sister worked as a servant for the wealthy Maza family. The Mazas also hired Benito. When Benito arrived in Oaxaca, he couldn't read or write, because he had never gone to school. He spoke only the Zapotec language of his village. But the head of the Maza family took note of Benito's intelligence and eagerness to learn. Under his master's guidance, Benito was soon reading and writing in Spanish and doing math. Benito even learned to make books by hand.

Benito entered a religious school to prepare to be a priest but later enrolled in the Institute of Science and Art, where he studied to be a lawyer. He then entered politics. Later he married Margarita Maza, the daughter of his teacher and benefactor.

Entre los individuos, como entre las naciones, el respeto al derecho ajeno es la paz.

Between individuals, as among nations,
respect for the rights of others is peace.
—Benito Juárez

Benito Juárez became governor of Oaxaca and later the chief justice of the Supreme Court. In 1861 he became president of Mexico, and in 1862 the French army invaded.

When the French took Mexico City in 1863, President Juárez and his government were forced to flee to the north. President Juárez led the opposition to the French-backed Emperor Maximilian of Austria. After four years of resistance by the Mexican people, pressure from the United States, and criticism within France, the French forces withdrew. In 1867 Emperor Maximilian was captured and sentenced to death by firing squad.

During his time in office Benito Juárez helped curtail the powers of the Catholic Church over the government of Mexico. Under new laws passed during his presidency, church property was taken over by the State for the benefit of all citizens. Throughout his time in office, President Juárez was dedicated to establishing equal rights for the nation's many native people. His example of leadership helps to ensure that Mexico will always be a free and independent nation.

The portrait of Benito Juárez appears on the 20-peso bill.

Mexican Immigrants Come to the United States

Like many Californians, Rosie's parents are immigrants from Mexico. After they married, they moved to the United States from Jalisco, one of Mexico's thirty-one states. Rosie's parents became citizens of the United States and have lived and worked in the San Francisco Bay area for more than twenty-five years.

Mexican immigrants and Americans of Mexican descent share a unique place in the history of the United States. They are among the oldest—and newest—inhabitants of the nation. Some Mexicans were already living in parts of the Southwest before it became a part of the United States. Others have arrived in recent years.

Mexican immigrants make up a large portion of the population in the United States today. According to the last census, there are 33.1 million immigrants in the United States and one third are from Mexico. It is likely that immigrants from Mexico will continue to add to the cultural richness of the United States for many years to come—influencing language, food, music, and culture.

Rosie enjoys talking on the phone to her friends as she walks home from school.

Rosie's father and her grandmother show her pictures of relatives who live in Jalisco, Mexico.

Rosie helps her mother and grandmother prepare enchiladas for a family meal. These enchiladas are vegetarian, served with tomato sauce and lots of cheese on top.

Immigration from Mexico to the Unites States has come in three large waves. The first was in the early part of the twentieth century, as hardships brought on by the Mexican Revolution pushed people north. Between 1910 and 1930, the number of Mexican immigrants tripled.

The second wave of immigration came as a result of World War II. In the 1940s, as part of a special Braceros program, more than 5 million people from Mexico were invited to come to the United States to work. These Mexicans took the place on farms and in factories of Americans who had gone to fight in the war. Many, such as Rosie's grandfather, stayed on after the war. Many brought their families to live in the United States.

Today, a third wave is bringing thousands of Mexicans across the border. In the 1960s immigration policies were changed to allow more people from the Southern Hemisphere to immigrate. In the 1990s more immigrants came legally from Mexico than from all European countries combined. Many of the newest immigrants, however, are unauthorized and undocumented. That means that they are coming to the United States without official permission from the US government. This remains one of the largest issues between the US and Mexico today.

A plate of enchiladas is surrounded by extra toppings: avocado, salsa, lemon, radishes, cabbage, and Mexican rice.

Sometimes Rosie helps out at her father's store.

Rosie's father and her uncles own a Mexican-style grocery store called El Porvenir. Many of their customers are immigrants from Mexico too. They are happy to find a place where it feels like home. Inside, there are bins full of fresh fruits and vegetables and shelves filled with dried herbs and spices, large bags of rice and beans, and cans of chiles.

The store offers many special services. There is a butcher shop, or *carnicería*. Watches and jewelry are for sale in the *joyería*. A *zapatería* offers shoes and boots for sale. Each morning, the *panadería* in the back of the store produces fresh breads and pastries. People can also cash checks or send money directly to their families in Mexico. High above everything, there are piñatas of every shape and size—perfect for a fiesta.

El Porvenir stocks many food items that are important in Mexican cooking: fresh tomatillos, yuca, chiles of every shape and description—and supersized Mexican papayas.

Tomatillos

Yuca

Chiles

carnicería

panadería

A carnicería is a store that sells meat.

A panadería is a store selling bread and sweets.

A zapatería is a store where you can buy shoes.

A joyería is a jewelry store.

zapatería

joyería

Elote Fresco
Mexican-style Corn on the Cob

1. Shuck the corn. Boil the ears of corn in salted water for 12 minutes.

or

Roast the corn on a barbecue with the husks on. Turn the ears every few minutes to cook on all sides. This takes about 12 minutes over medium heat. Remove the husks.

2. Spread the boiled or roasted corn with butter and then sprinkle with chile molido. Add some *queso cotija* and season with a squeeze of lime juice.

¡Qué sabrosa! It's absolutely delicious!

Outside the store Ana González sells homemade tamales and slices of mango with lime. On cold mornings she makes a drink made of chocolate and cornmeal called *atole*. When it is in season, Rosie likes *elote*, a Mexican-style corn-on-the-cob treat.

11

Learning About Mexican Culture

Although Rosie is growing up far from Mexico, she is learning about Mexican culture and traditions. Some days after school, Rosie goes to a youth center called Los Cenzontles to learn about Mexican music and dance.

Rosie started coming to the center when she was eight years old. Her older sister María saw a flyer about classes there. She knew Rosie would enjoy them and learn something at the same time. Rosie started out in dance classes, but soon added singing. Now she is studying the violin too.

At first Rosie was shy about speaking Spanish at the center. Although her parents speak Spanish at home, Rosie goes to school with kids who only speak English. At the center she met other kids who have parents from Mexico. She could practice speaking Spanish with the teachers and the other kids—and that gave her confidence.

(Above) Los Cenzontles is a place where kids can learn about Mexican music and traditions.

(Right) Victor, one of Rosie's friends at the center, joins his grandfather, who is visiting from Mexico.

Mariachi–The Music of Mexico

Rosie and the other kids who come to learn about Mexican culture at Los Cenzontles have very good teachers. One of these is Julián González Saldaña, a professional mariachi from Jalisco, Mexico.

No one really knows where the term "mariachi" comes from. As Julián González tells it, the first mariachis were workers on the haciendas of Old Mexico. A hacienda is a large ranch where people grow crops or raise cattle and sheep. The work was always hard—*muy duro*.

At the end of the day, when the workers wanted to relax, they had to make their own entertainment. In those days there were no televisions or movie theaters. Instead, people gathered around with their instruments. They made music together and danced. This is how the mariachis first got started.

Traditional mariachis used instruments that were introduced to Mexico by the Spanish—such as the harp, violin, and *vihuela*. Mariachi music, however, is a blend of many different influences.

In addition to playing instruments, the mariachis also sang. They sang about their heroes and about bandits who roamed the highways. Some songs told about events that were happening in the country. These became a way for people to keep up with the latest news. Sometimes mariachis sang about birds and animals. Julián's favorite tune is called *"El Guaco."* In this song he copies the call of a bird that lives in Jalisco. It is so funny and lifelike, people always laugh.

Mariachi music begins with a *son,* or rhythm. Each region in Mexico has a particular son that comes from a popular dance. A son from Chiapas is different from a son from Jalisco. Since the songs of the mariachi are based on a rhythm, they can go on and on. Julián González remembers that on the ranches, songs could last for ten or twenty minutes. The mariachis improvised the lyrics to a song, ending only when the dancers were too tired to go on.

The songs the mariachis played were very expressive. A crowd listening to the music could hear different things. The songs are poetic. They can mean different things to different people.

Julián González is a mariachi musician from Jalisco who teaches at Los Cenzontles Mexican Arts Center.

Rosie and a few other students look at a new CD that the group has produced.

13

The number of musicians in a mariachi band can vary—sometimes there are as many as twenty. Usually a band will consist of two trumpets, two violins, one Spanish guitar (*guitarra de golpe*), one vihuela, and one *guitarrón* (shown above). Most of the musicians who play in a mariachi band can also sing.

The guitarrón makes a unique sound and is sometimes called *el alma del mariachi*—the soul of the mariachi.

Mariachi music changed from local folk tradition to popular music during the 1920s, when Girilo Marmolejo brought his mariachi group from Tecolotlán in Jalisco to Mexico City. They played in what is now the Plaza Garibaldi.

After the Revolution of 1910, mariachi music became a symbol of the Mexican nation. Since then, Mexican presidents have used mariachi music for political events. In 1933 Girilo Marmolejo led the first international tour of mariachis to the Chicago World's Fair in the United States and made a recording with Columbia Records.

In the beginning, mariachis wore the same clothes that they wore to work on the ranches—homespun cotton pants and a shirt, a simple straw hat, and handmade sandals called *huaraches*. When they began to play for presidents and make records, their clothing changed too.

In 1934 President Lázaro Cárdenas invited a group called Mariachi Vargas de Tecalitlán to play at his inauguration. Some say that the president asked the mariachis to wear *traje de charro*, the clothing of Jalisco's *charros*, or cowboys. Today, many mariachis wear the short charro jacket over tight-fitting trousers and short riding boots. The jacket and pants are often covered with intricate embroidery and silver buttons. Like the charros, the mariachis wear large sombreros.

String instruments such as the guitar, the violin, and the harp were used to make traditional mariachi music. The trumpet is a modern addition. It's strong, brassy sound is what many people associate with the mariachi style today. The inventions of the phonograph, radio, and cinema helped popularize mariachi music. Today, mariachi music has become one of Mexico's national symbols.

Rosie and Victor practice a style of dancing called *zapateado*.

One of Rosie's friends helps her get ready for the performance.

In Mexico today, mariachi music is an important part of any celebration. Mariachis are present at festivals, baptisms, weddings, and other celebrations. In Mexico mariachis can often be found in the zócalo, the main plaza in the center of a town. Anyone can hire the mariachi to play, and they still charge by the song.

At Los Cenzontles, Julián González and the other teachers are trying to re-create a time when playing music was a part of everyday life. Regardless of which instruments are used—whether traditional mariachi with only string instruments or a modern band with lots of brass—it is still the songs that matter. These songs tell about real people and their hopes and dreams. The songs we hear today connect us with the real people who lived so long ago.

(Below) Victor and other young people from Los Cenzontles perform a traditional Mexican dance.

This unusual instrument is called a *quijada*—because it is made from the lower jaw of a horse or donkey.

(Above right) Eugene Rodríguez, the founder and director of Los Cenzontles Mexican Arts Center, is a third-generation Mexican American. Eugene has dedicated his life to bringing traditional Mexican music to the Hispanic communities of Northern California.

(Above left) Rosie joins other young people in the group to sing a *ranchera*, a traditional song of the Mexican countryside.

(Below left) Victor and Rosie perform a zapateado.

17

Celebrating Cinco de Mayo

Finally Cinco de Mayo is here. After school the kids from Los Cenzontles climb into vans and travel to a small town on the coast of California. Just like the mariachis of Old Mexico, the kids will travel to share Mexican music, dance, and song.

Their group has been invited to a fiesta in the town of Point Reyes, California. Many of the people who live in Point Reyes work on farms and in dairies. Many are immigrants from Mexico. The fiesta takes place in Toby's Feed Barn, a place where people come to buy hay and feed for their livestock. The event is free for everyone in the community.

(Below) Victor, his father, and his younger brother wait for the fiesta to begin.

(Right) Rosie and her friends enjoy a quick dinner before the performance.

(Above) Toby's Feed Barn, decorated with *papel picado*, fills with people eager to hear the concert as part of their Cinco de Mayo celebration.

(Left) Rosie's teachers Fabiola and Lucina sing a ranchera with Julián González. They are wearing traditional shawls called *rebozos*. Julián González and the other musicians wear the peasant clothing of traditional mariachis.

19

El Torero

Mamá, me quiero casar,
Pero ha de ser
    con un torero,
Pa'que me saque
    a pasear
Y me dé mucho dinero.

¡Ay, mamita, sí!
¡Ay, mamita, no!
Que se va, que se va,
Y ya nunca volverá.

Mamá, me quiero casar,
Pero ha de ser
    con un torero
Que sepa banderillear
Y ganar mucho dinero.

Ya no quiero
    a Manga Mocha,
Ni tampoco
    a Cuatro Dedos;
El que quiero
    es a Turincio,
Que es el rey
    de los toreros.

At the Cinco de Mayo celebration Victor and Rosie perform a dance called
El Torero. The boy dances the part of the bull, *el toro*. The girl is the *torero*, or
bullfighter. In the song a girl asks her mother to let her marry a bullfighter so she
will be rich and famous one day. Rosie uses her shawl as a bullfighter's cape.

20

The Bullfighter

Mama, I want to get married,
But it's going to be
    with a bullfighter,
So he'll take me out
And give me lots of money.

Oh, mama, yes!
Oh, mama, no!
He's leaving, he's leaving,
And he'll never come back.

Mama, I want to get married,
But it has to be
    with a bullfighter
Who'll know how
    to use the banderillas
And earn a lot of money.

I don't want the
    one-armed bullfighter,
Nor the one with four fingers;
I want Turincio,
Who is the king
    of the bullfighters.

The children from the West Marin School helped to make this Cinco de Mayo celebration special. Each class learned a different traditional dance from Mexico.

21

Lucina and Jorge dance on the tarima, *a portable wooden platform. The tarima amplifies the sound of the dancing feet.*

The evening begins with traditional mariachi music, and the kids take turns showing the crowd many different dances. Rosie and her friends demonstrate the quick steps of a dance called zapateado. The word *zapatos* means "shoes," and this dance features the sound of a dancer's heels striking the floor to make a rhythm that complements the music. Some say the most important instruments in a mariachi band are the feet of the dancers.

Celebrating in the Community

(Left) Rosie and her sister Zoila learn more about registering to vote.

(Below) On Cinco de Mayo there are lots of Mexican flags for sale. For many immigrants the flag shows pride in their Mexican heritage.

Cinco de Mayo is a good time for communities to express their pride. Many cities in the San Francisco Bay area have large Hispanic populations, and many residents are immigrants from Mexico. In San Pablo a local church sponsors a festival of Mexican music, food, and entertainment.

Dance Groups

Crowds of People

Charros Performing with Lariat

Sombreros and Folkloric Clothing

A Cinco de Mayo Parade

For more than twenty years there has been a Cinco de Mayo parade in San Jose, California. A showcase of the best in Mexican American traditions, each year it gets bigger and better.

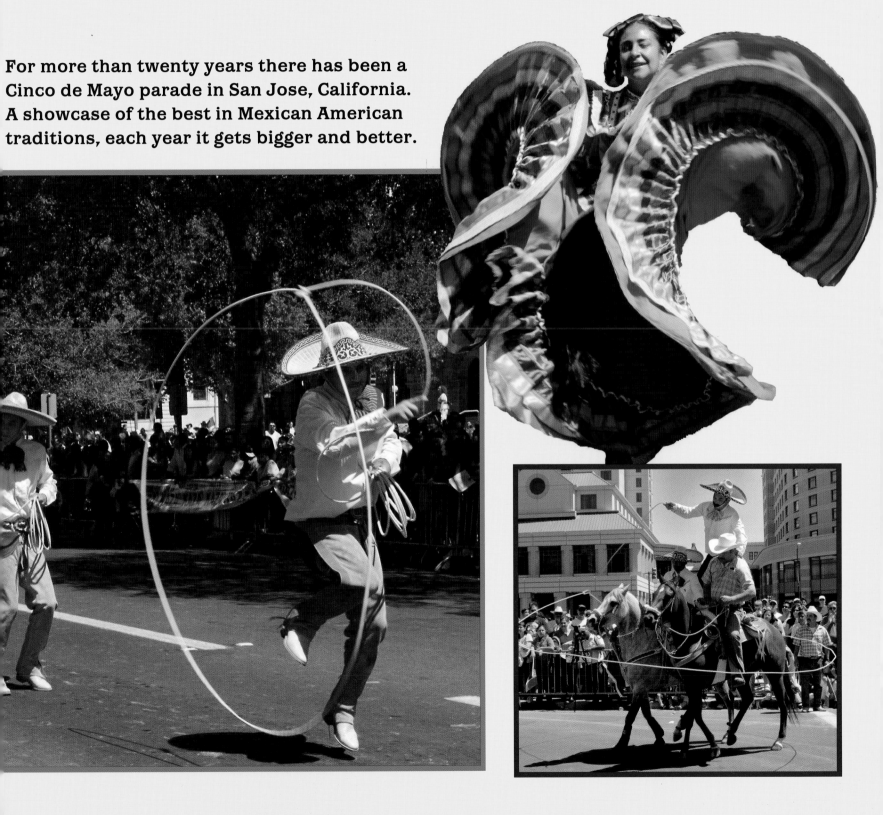

Classic Cars and Politicians

Charros and Charritos

Dancing Horses

A Festival of Mexican Food and Music

A Family Celebration

After the parades are over, Rosie and her family have more to celebrate. Cinco de Mayo is special for her family because it is the birthday of Rosie's grandmother. Rosie's aunts and her uncle and some of her cousins join the family for a *barbacoa* in the backyard. Rosie's mom grills *carne asada* on the barbecue. Everyone brings a dish to add to the meal. There is a salad made of cactus called *nopales*, as well as *frijoles* and *arroz mexicano*. At the end of the meal, Rosie's *abuelita* cuts a big *tres leches* cake, and they all sing *"Feliz Cumpleaños."*

Cinco de Mayo is a wonderful way to celebrate Mexican culture and traditions. But for Rosie, the best part comes when she can spend a day with her family. As they say at Rosie's house, *¡Viva México!* and most important, *¡Viva la familia!*

Rosie joins her sister María, her nephew, and her cousins in wishing her grandmother a very happy birthday.

28

Glossary of Spanish Words

abuelita, abuelito: grandmother, grandfather

arroz mexicano: rice cooked with chiles and tomatoes

atole: a hot drink made with cornmeal. Sometimes other flavors, such as chocolate, are added.

barbacoa: barbecue

bracero: guest worker from Mexico

calle 5 de Mayo: 5th of May Street

carne asada: beef cooked on a barbecue

carnicería: a shop where people can buy meat

charro: cowboy

chile molido: plain ground chile without any additives

Cinco de Mayo: Fifth of May

criollo: a person born in Mexico whose parents were born in Spain

el alma del mariachi: the soul of the mariachi

elote fresco: fresh corn on the cob

el porvenir: the future

enchilada: a popular Mexican dish made with tortillas, various fillings, salsa, and cheese

familia: family

Feliz Cumpleaños: Happy Birthday

fiesta: party

frijoles: beans

guitarra de golpe: a type of guitar found in Jalisco and Michoacán and used for rhythmic and chordal accompaniment in traditional music; also called a *jarana*

guitarrón: a large bass instrument used in traditional Mexican music

hacienda: a large ranch or farm

huaraches: handmade sandals worn by the peasants in Mexico

jarana: a small guitar with eight strings carved from a single piece of wood, also called *guitarra de golpe*

joyería: a store where one can buy watches and jewelry

los cenzontles: the mockingbirds

los indígenas: native people who have lived in a place for many thousands of years

machete: a long blade used to cut tall grasses and sugarcane

mariachi: a band of musicians who play the traditional songs of Mexico

mestizo: a person of mixed race; in Mexico, a person whose parents are Spanish and indigenous

muy duro: very hard

nopales: a type of eatable cactus used in Mexican cooking and eaten as a vegetable

panadería: a store where one can buy baked goods such as bread and pastries

papel picado: decorative cut paper

peso: a unit of money in Mexico, equal to about 10 cents in US currency

pueblo: a small town

qué sabrosa: how delicious

queso cotija: a dry, aged cheese similar to Parmesan cheese

quijada: percussion instrument made from the jaw of a horse or donkey, scraped with a thin stick along the teeth in the jaw and struck with a closed fist to give a distinctive rattling sound

rancheras: songs that are sung on the ranches of Mexico

rebozo: a traditional shawl worn by Mexican women

salsa: a spicy sauce made from various vegetables and fruit combinations

son (sones): a basic rhythm of traditional Mexican folk music

tarima: a small wooden platform used as a surface for traditional Mexican dances

tía, tío: aunt, uncle

traje de charro: clothing of the Mexican cowboys

tres leches: the name of a favorite cake made with three kinds of milk

vihuela: a guitarlike instrument that was very popular in sixteenth-century Spain, similar to the lute

zapateado: a traditional dance of Mexico, named for the technique of using the dancer's heels to tap out a rhythm or counterpoint to the music

zapatería: a store where one can buy shoes and boots

Zapotec: a language spoken by a group of indigenous people living in the central Mexican state of Oaxaca

zócalo: main square located in the center of many Mexican cities and towns

Index

Page numbers in italics refer to illustrations.

Mexico, divided into thirty-one states, is a land of many cultures. Although Spanish is the main language spoken in Mexico, many indigenous groups speak their own languages. Each region of the country has different foods, music, and dances.

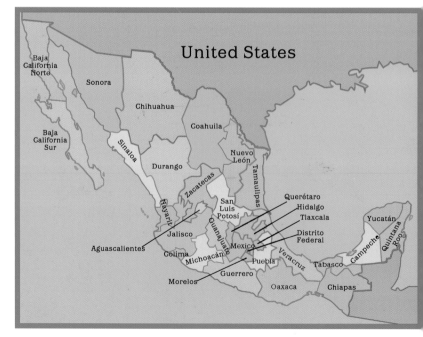